So You Think...

615-543-1557

SO YOU THINK...

You Know Church Folks?

Prophetess Paula Ferguson

Rev. date: 05/04/2022

To order additional copies of this book, contact:
Xlibris
844-714-8691
www.Xlibris.com
Orders@Xlibris.com
820772

Church folk will Bless you out and then REPENT!
It doesn't mean they aren't saved
You just caught em' on
THE WRONG DAY!

CONTENTS

A NOTE FROM THE AUTHOR

Dear Reader:

I appreciate you purchasing this power-packed book and believe in my heart that God will use the words within these pages to heal your wounded spirit.

I decree that this book will encourage your fainting heart and lift your bowed head. Everyone has a story. It's up to you to decide who gets to listen. Everyone has a sad song; choose wisely your key.

You will notice the last pages of this book are blank. As you read and see yourself or are reminded of an experience in your past, take time to write them down. I want you to do four things:

1. Make a list of every hurtful encounter you have experienced and can remember.
2. Reflect on how much you have survived.
3. Make a covenant between yourself and God that you will never allow these hurtful events to affect you ever again—signing it and dating it—this is a spiritual contract. (A written covenant is a sure covenant—Nehemiah 9:38.)

4. Scripture says in 1 Peter 5:7, "*Casting all your care upon him; for HE careth for you.*" As an act of casting away every hurt, disappointment, offense, and injustice, tear your list out and send them to me for one of my upcoming series: "So You Think . . . You've Been Hurt."

Those whose testimonials are used in the book will receive an autographed copy of the book. Send all correspondence to the following address:

Paula Ferguson Ministries
pfergusonministries@outlook.com
AGAIN, THANK YOU FOR YOUR CONTINUED SUPPORT.
SHALOM!

-PROPHETESS PAULA FERGUSON

ABOUT THE AUTHOR

As I began to revisit my own personal testimonies, understanding the scripture that says, "And they overcame him by the blood of the Lamb and by the word of their testimony . . . " (Revelation 12:11), I realized I had suffered many hardships, disappointments, abuse, betrayals, and neglect at the hands of their spiritual leaders and realized that Father God had ordained their pain for such a time as this to heal the wounds that are prevalent in the body of Christ.

Through nothing but THE UNADULTERATED WORD OF GOD, and spending intimate time with Father I continue to heal.

ABOUT THIS BOOK

The *So You Think . . .* series will expose the betrayals and delve into the deep waters no one is willing to confront.

Who will shout, "The emperor has no clothes?" What do you do when your pastor is the pedophile, your protector becomes your abuser, and your spiritual covering could care less?

Does sin really stink in the nostrils of God? The reader will find comfort in knowing that Father IS concerned and He IS just. He loves us, though He must balance His compassion with judgment that all may experience His unconditional love.

So You Think . . . will MAKE you think!

To my loving husband
Craig John Ferguson.

"You are MY proof that GOD WAS INDEED LISTENING."

"I love you with all my heart, honey."

-Paula

FOREWORD

Our lives are filled with challenges and difficulties as we move from one stage of maturity to another. There are situations many will encounter that require relational accountability to facilitate getting over whatever human weakness may manifest as an outcome of incorrect organizational, immature leadership, and crossing moral boundaries.

Some years ago, there was a division of a large corporation in the news. The president of the division had tried many times to get leadership to take accountability and address significant issues yet was unsuccessful. The division's president knew that if it was not dealt with, these problems would eventually break down the company.

As things continued to worsen, the division president leaked the issues to the press in an effort to put external pressure on and to force its company to deal with its problems.

The moral of this situation is there will be times when you will be required to escalate and put bad situations on the table, which may include sharing details of intimate, internal problems most would prefer kept from the public.

That company president's intent was not to destroy the company through exposure; rather, it was done with the mindset and hope that the exposure will promote an increased willingness to fix the problems!

This is what you are about to get in the book *So You Think You Know Church Folks?*

In this book, you will read about exposures, which come from different situations within some local churches.

Some of you reading this book may say "something similar happened in my church," or "that happened in my congregation," or even "I've heard of that happening at this church or at that church." This is because these are not isolated issues. The details revealed in this book are not isolated to one particular church or location.

I would suggest that situations like those discussed in this book can happen almost anywhere across the entire western hemisphere, if not the entire world, regardless of ethnicity, race, or gender.

You are challenged as you read this book to not become so overly concerned about the language used by the characters; rather, it is to observe what happens when amoral problems within church organizations present themselves and are not addressed according to the word of God.

This book is simply the writer's perspective on the fallout, the damage, the hurt, and the injuries that are a consequence of the unwillingness to address serious issues and, at the end, an invitation to begin the process of healing for those who have been involved in similar situations.

I challenge you to read this book with this in mind: Sometimes exposure has to take place in order for healing to *begin*. There has to be a willingness to hear from God when it's time to expose certain things. Once put out on the table, we are now forced to look at it, learn from it, make the appropriate changes, and live.

Get ready to *enjoy this book*!

Apostle Craig J. Ferguson

INTRODUCTION

How are you all doing out there? I've been told I need to introduce this book. I rightly don't know what to say to you, except everything you are about to read is the truth. I'm here to tell the truth, the whole truth, and nothing but the truth, so help me God.

Now, if you one of those touchy so-called church folk, let me say, I'm not about to start apologizing. We've got babies out there who won't half listen to the word of God because of all the foolishness going on in the church. A person can't even live saved these days.

When you think about it, the truth needs no proof; either it is or it ain't. This book isn't about real saints but folks who "ain't." Come on now, you know what I'm talking about—saved on Sunday and AIN'T on Monday. Tell the truth and shame the devil!

Now let me stop to thank all the folks out there who helped bring this book to pass. If it hadn't been for you lying on me, backbiting, and trying to hold a sista back, you would never have pissed me off enough to write this book. I know why you're mad. You're mad because you know I'm not lying. I'm telling the truth on you. ***But you'll get over it***.

Now to all you good Christian folk out there, don't change because the kingdom needs more folk like you. But let me say this: Momma's never bit her tongue, and I ain't about to start now just to appease you. So I hope you don't get easily offended. This is some strong meat. So don't choke.

Thank you, babies. Bye now.

—**Mother Mattie Gill**

CHAPTER 1

Watch Out for Those Snakes!

"Baby, first, you've got to understand how church folks is, and second, you've got to try your best not to become one of the those damn snakes! Now I'm not talking about saved or Christian folks, honey. I'm talking about . . . well, have a seat, take a load off. Let me give you an example of what I mean . . . It was just a few years ago when all this that I'm talking about happened. We were having one of our church functions when all of a sudden, child . . ."

"Giving honor to God who is the head of my life. I just want to start off by saying that I almost didn't make it this morning. You see, Satan tried to stop me, but he didn't win!"

Quietly, the entire church listened as Sister King told her testimony. I had heard it all before myself, when something happened that changed my whole outlook on being called a Christian.

"You need to sit your lying ass down right now before I sit it down for you!"

Eyes bucked from every area of the church as Pastor stood erect and shouted, "Ladies, ladies, ladies! This is the house of God!"

Turning her attention to Pastor Peters, Sister Hamilton began to cry. "And don't even try to stand there and say shit to me because I'm sick of your ass too!" Shouting at the top of her voice, "TELL HER! AND I MEAN TELL HER NOW, OR I WILL! YOU HEAR ME? I SWEAR I WILL!"

It was then that the scripture containing the words "ITCHING EARS" came to mind. I saw people who normally fell asleep every Sunday like clockwork wide awake, listening to every word that came from the pulpit.

Immediately, members of the deacon board rushed to a very upset and outraged Sister Hamilton, forcefully taking her to the back of the church and right out of the side door.

Now you know that Pastor and Retta King have been doing the dirty for about a year now, and everybody knows about Quetta Hamilton. I guess he must have a thing for the "-ettas," if you know what I mean. Anyhow, Quetta found out about Retta, and all hell broke loose.

See, even though Retta found out about Quetta, Retta really didn't give a damn because she used to say, "If a man will cheat on his wife for you, then he will cheat on you for someone else." However, Quetta wasn't even having that. I don't know why all these stupid tail women keep falling for the same mess because you not gone ever be the first lady when the lights are on—HE'LL TELL YOU ANYTHING WHEN THE LIGHTS ARE OFF! Anyhow, before they could get Quetta to the back pew, she up and yelled at him, "Your dumb ass gave me AIDS! This shit ain't over!"

Right then and there, about five other females stood up and screamed, "What! You son of a bitch!" That's when it got good.

Why you got that look on your face, child? Stuff like this happens every day, so don't be surprised. Hell, as nice as you look, I'm shocked Pastor didn't take a go at you. Child, you know, he even tried to take a drink of THIS here tall cool liquid, but you know Momma wasn't having it, although he WAS drunk and crying at the time.

Anyway, you're probably wondering where Sister Peters was during all this. Well, she was sitting where she always is, on the front row to the right, with her fan in one hand and her Bible in the other. You know women of God need to stop being so damn ignorant. How are you going to let a whore take your man? You're sitting there rocking back and forth, praying and rebuking the devil, when you need to be doing one of two things: either casting that whore devil out or beating the devil out that WHORE! Now you're mad because I told you the truth!

When you get finished being mad at Momma, you're going to find out that I'm right. As a matter of fact, I don't even care because, after eighty-seven years of living on this planet, I seen some stuff to make you cry, and I still haven't finished my assignment because of negroes like the ones I'm talking about! Let me get back to my story.

Lady Peters, not too long ago, found out she had cancer and has been moving kind of slow here lately. You know, I feel right sorry for the girl because she's only been married a few years. She's so young too! But a whore is going to be a whore, and that girl married herself a whore! Looks like to me the cancer got worse after she got with that fool. He's up here calling himself a pastor, talking about he's just like his spiritual father Apax. Now I knew Apostle Apax, and he surely wasn't a whore.

In fact, if there ever was a true man of God, I KNOW it was him. I believe the Lord truly walked with that man. I just don't know where Peters went wrong. After Apax died, he just started sleeping with everything that had a tail, and I do mean EVERYTHING! Girls and boys from what I hear. That Peters ain't right! Look here, hold on for a minute, my phone is ringing. I'll be right back. Lord, I wonder who that is calling this time of morning?

"Hello . . . Hey, baby. Can you hold on for a minute?"

Walking back outside to the porch, Mother Gill realizes she needs to get rid of her visitor so she can gossip. So she sends her down to the corner store. "Look, take this twenty, and run down to the corner store, and get me some chops. And tell Jerry not to be putting his thumb on the scale either because it's for Mother Gill down the way. That way, he won't try to cheat you none. All right, when you get back, I'm gonna cook us some lunch . . ."

Returning to the phone, Mother Gill eases into her rocker, preparing herself for a little friendly who-shot-john. "Sorry about that, sweetie. How are you feeling? Better, I hope. I know it's been a real trial, hasn't it? The baby okay? Good. You know I was just thinking about you and what happened a while back. It's something that you called when you did. How much more weight have you lost? Well, that's good. It slowed down some. Have you found anybody to take Mordecai?

Well, you know, if I wasn't so old, I would, but I can just barely take care of myself with the help of the Lord. Now refresh my memory again—exactly what happened to make you act so damn foolish anyhow? You KNOW your momma raised you better than that, and if she had been their girl, seeing them cart you out of the church, she would have just died all over again . . . right after slapping the hell out of both you and the pastor. How you let that man under your skin any way, huh?"

"Ma Gill, you just don't know how much I really loved that man. Terry really had me believing that he was going to marry me once Trish died. I know, I know. It's wrong, but once that man got inside my head, it was hard to know just who was doing the thinking."

Thinking how could anyone be this stupid, Mother Gill responds out loud, "Child, hasn't anybody ever told you if a man can get in your head, he can get between your legs? And once he's between your legs, it's hard to get him out of your bed!"

"It does me a lot of good for you to tell me now. You should have said something sooner! You know, I never told anybody what I am about to tell you. I didn't even tell Momma before she died. The day I joined the church, I remember him telling me that the Lord showed me to him, standing in the sanctuary, dressed in pink, and said that I was his next wife. Damn, I was so stupid!"

"Honey, don't stress yourself too much about it 'cause you've got bastards out there calling themselves people of God, and they're doing more shit than sinners. You know, even when Jesus spoke about sinners, He only called THEM ungodly. In fact, I believe the worst thing He ever called any unsaved person was when He called

Herod a fox. But now, baby, let me tell you, when He talked about us, church folks, He called us snakes!"

"I guess you're right because as much as you cuss, I sometimes wonder about you!"

"Believe me when I tell you, Quetta, cussing is the last thing that's going to keep me out of heaven. If there's nothing you can do to buy your way in, there's not too much you can do to buy your way out. It's in the word. That's why Terry has me so worked up because he's got all these people down there following his example, and he knows he ain't right!"

Listening to Mother Gill, Quetta started crying and said, "You know, Momma, one day I went to his house while his wife was at chemo, and I caught him in a compromising situation!"

Clearing her voice, she said, "What do you mean, with that funny fella?"

"Yeah! How did you know?"

"There's not too much Momma don't know, baby. I knew when you started spreading your legs like the Red Sea. I just never said anything because I felt like you were grown and you knew what you were doing. Seeing how things turned out, now I wish I would have said something to you because now look at you. Now you're sick with AIDS, and you've got a sick child to boot by a man who ain't even worth shit!"

"Momma, you've got to stop all that cussin'!"

Standing in her doorway, Mother Gill noticed her company was drawing close. Bringing her conversation to an end, with her hand on her hips as if Quetta was standing right in front of her, she said, "Girl, every word I've said is in the Bible, including shit. As a matter of fact, the Bible calls it 'shittum.' That's what's wrong with saints today, they get caught up on the little mess and miss God all together. I've got to go now. Come by and see me Wednesday. I'll be able to talk more then. Okay? Bye now . . ."

Hanging up the phone, there's a knock at the door. "Child, what took you so long? I thought for sure you had slaughtered the pig and chopped him up! Anyhow, come on in so I can fry up these chops . . ."

CHAPTER 2

This Here Has Got to Stop!

Riding along in his car, it seemed what had just happened back at the church had no effect on Terry whatsoever. It was as if it boosted his ego just knowing he was behind so much pain. How could this perversion have slithered into the heart of this man of God? Suddenly, his phone rings, and he notices from the caller ID that it's Deacon Randall.

Terry answers, "It's your dime, so don't waste my time—run your mouth!"

"Watch out there now! What was all that mess about? You can't keep your whores under control, man?"

Laughing, Terry responds, "Oh, don't be deceived now. Trust me, if there's one thing this player knows, a REAL PLAYER can't get played playing his OWN game! Okay . . ."

There once was a time when Deac Randal would never have fathomed the idea of having such a carnal conversation with a man of God, but a little leaven leavens the whole lump. Terry's perverted thinking, in a very short time, had totally transformed the minds of even the faithful few who remained at the church after Apostle Apax passed on into eternity.

Back at the church, Trish is waiting for the finance committee to finish up. She walks into Terry's office to find he has already left. "Dang, he could have at least let me know that he was leaving."

Preparing to leave his office, Trish notices he left his notepad sitting out on his desk. This was a "NO, NO" for Terry, seeing he forbade her to touch, let alone read it, when they're at home. Curiosity was killing the cat. "Well, I can't leave his office like this. I've got to at least straighten his desk." She lies to herself.

Walking over to his desk, she notices Terry has jotted down several appointments for the following day:

1. Special counseling session with Deamon – 6:00 a.m.
2. Special counseling session with Demetta – 8:15 a.m.
3. Meeting with Deacon Randall – 10:00 a.m. (take lots of cash)
4. Call Trish (whenever)
5. Return Dr. Clayborn's phone call?

What was all this scribbling about? Why so many appointments in one day? Preparing to sit down and thumb through the notepad, there's a knock at the office door.

"Baby, you all right in there?" It was Mother Gill.

Unlocking the door, Trish invites her in and closes the door behind her. Offering her a seat, Trish leans on the desk.

"Mother, I was on my way out. Terry just left."

With a knowing in her voice, Mother Gill replies, "Oh, he did, did he? How long has that sucker been gone?"

Trying her best to muster up a look of innocence, Trish calmly says, "Oh, you just missed him. He hasn't even been gone five minutes."

Grabbing her purse off her lap, Mother Gill stands with her hand on one hip and says, "Now I may be a fool, but I sure as hell ain't a damn fool. That boy's been gone for over an hour. Why are you lying for him?"

Looking down in shame, Trish sheepishly replies, "Well, Mother, I was ashamed to admit that my own husband doesn't regard me enough to speak to me in the morning. So why should I expect him to let me know that he left the church?"

"Are you sure you heard from God? I mean, are you SURE he said 'THIS MAN' was your husband?"

Trish responds, "Yes, I'm sure, Mother. I asked Him if this man was my husband."

"What did he say?"

"He said, 'You'll know.'"

Looking at her with disbelief in her eyes, Mother emphatically replies, "Naw, baby. What He actually said was 'HELL NO!' Now, I ain't trying to sow a seed of discord, but after what happened here this morning, he needs to be havin' his behind here, licking you all up and down your spine, begging for forgiveness. I don't see how you put up with it."

In an effort to hide her tears, Trish reaches behind her and grabs Terry's notepad. Handing it to Mother Gill, she explains, "There was a message from Dr. Clayborn, and Terry never even mentioned that he'd called. Should I return Dr. Clayborn's call, or should I wait for Terry to give me the message?"

Heading toward the door, with the notepad in her hand, Mother says, "Should you call him? SHOULD YOU CALL HIM? Why in the hell SHOULDN'T you call him? Ain't that YOUR doctor? Why should you have to wait for Terry to come back to the church to give you a message that you've got in your hand right now? I'll fix this. UM gonna call him."

Panicking, Trish lunges for the pad, saying, "No! Terry will be mad if he knew that I was even in his office without his permission."

Yanking away from her, leaning back on one leg, Mother Gill abruptly responds, "Do you see a look of 'I'm scared of that bastard' on my face? Now I said um gonna call. And if he asks about this darn notepad, you just send him on over to 8925 Emily Circle. Tell him **I said** to climb the stairs, ring my doorbell, and to **PLEASE** make sure he ain't got no liquid in his bladder. Cos I'm gone politely proceed to step outside on **MY** porch and beat the hell out of him. You're the one that's gotta sleep with him. I don't."

Sadly, Trish responds, "And I don't even get to do that."

Slamming the door, Mother Gill says, "Now THAT's your fault. Don't complain about what you can change."

Though Mother Gill continues to fuss, Trish's mind drifts away to an incident that had happened just days before. Terry had pulled one of his disappearing acts and left her alone at the house. While getting ready to go to the gym, the phone begins to ring. Ignoring the ring, Trish continues to dress, knowing her exercise class would start soon. Finally, the annoying rings stop. But then there's a knock at the door.

Standing with a smile on his face, with his ear to his cell phone, to Trish's surprise, was Bishop Allen. Jokingly, he says, "I'm glad I wasn't Jesus calling you."

Trying to hold her composure and the trembling in her voice, Trish apologizes for not answering the phone and asks if he would like to come in. Bishop Allen, in all respect, was the finest man Trish had ever seen. He was LITERALLY tall, dark, **and** handsome; six-foot even, with the spirit to match; clean-shaven, clean cut, and just plain clean.

"I noticed that Pastor Peters's car was not in the driveway, so I was calling to see when you expected him to return."

"Terry left several hours ago to attend the superintendent's meeting with all the district pastors. He should be back soon, assuming no one wants to preach. You know how it is when you get a lot of preachers in one room, someone's bound to start preaching. But you're welcome to come in and wait."

Accepting her offer of kindness, Bishop Allen enters the house but goes no further than the chair by the door. He notices her duffel bag on the floor and the fact that she is wearing sports gear. Trying not to stare, something else becomes very apparent to Quentin that he had never noticed before. Trish was stunningly beautiful outside of her traditional church attire. Being a pastor's wife, Trish always dressed very conservatively, revealing very little. With her makeup perfectly applied and her shoulder-length hair always pulled up in a bun, her handmade hats only concealed her natural beauty even more.

The absence of these things only made her more beautiful. Before he'd realized what was taking place, Quentin found himself gazing at her. "Bishop, Bishop, are you okay? Is something wrong?"

Snapping back into reality, he responds, "Oh, I'm sorry, First Lady, my mind drifted there for a moment."

Feeling awkward, Trish thought it would be best if she changed attire, so she excuses herself. "I'm going to step in the back for just a moment to change, Bishop, I'll be right back!"

Realizing the inconvenience he was causing, he stands to leave and responds, "You don't have to do that on my account. Just ask Pastor Peters to call me when he gets in. He mentioned that he wanted me to minister this Sunday."

Grabbing his arm, Trish tells him, "Don't leave, I mean, um, I will only be a moment, and Terry should be home soon. To be honest with you, I am enjoying the company."

Rushing to the bedroom, Trish proceeds to look for something a little less form-fitting. She had to find something Terry would approve of, so she grabs one of his jogging suits out of the closet and throws it on. *This is perfect*, she thought. *It is just big enough to hide EVERYTHING, and if Terry were to walk in, he would think nothing of it!*

Agreeing to stay, Bishop Allen says a prayer in his heart. *Father, you said that you would not put more on us than we could bare, give me strength, and* PLEASE *help me make a covenant with my eyes because—*taking a deep breath—*this is one of the most gracefully attractive women that I've ever met.*

It was true, there was something about Trish that made her irresistible inside and out to everyone who entered her presence, it was her spirit.

Trish was such a very humble person who only wanted to please the Lord. She would often analyze herself to ensure she was representing her husband to the best of her ability.

Back in the sitting room, Bishop Allen feels his flesh rising and decides not to give space to the devil. What was happening to him? He could not explain it. This had NEVER happened before when he was around Trish in the past. Speaking loud enough for Trish to hear in the back, he says, "I'm going to be leaving now, just tell Pastor that I came by. I'll see you at church."

Breaking for the door before she could make it back up front, Quentin dashes out the front door to his car. Backing out of the driveway, he begins to thank God he was not the man he used to be.

Trish had to admit she was glad he was gone. It had been a long time since a man had made her feel like a schoolgirl, and she was not about to allow the enemy to set her up. Down on the inside, she knew this was a test and that she had passed.

Are you listening to me, child? Raising her voice, Mother Gill shouts, "HELLO! Is anybody home?"

All at once, Trish realizes she is in Terry's office, being chewed out by Mother Gill for allowing him to treat her so bad.

"Look, how are you supposed to get home anyway?"

"Actually, I was going to ask if you wouldn't mind giving me a lift." Somehow Mother Gill knew this was coming and was already prepared.

The ride home was tense, and Trish could feel her chest tightening up the closer she got to the house. Would Terry be there? She knew she would have to deal with what happened at the church today. Remembering what Terry had asked her to do earlier was making her stomach ball up in knots. It would be hours before Terry came home.

This had been the longest week for Trish. Sitting on the foot of the bed, she began to weep as things began to run across her mind. Softly, she began to talk to the Lord. "Father, I have tried so hard to please You, but I feel like You have forgotten me. Why me, Lord? Why? This man's been so mean to me, and all I ever wanted to do was love him. When I asked You for my soul mate, I met Terry and felt like it would be okay. I had somebody to love. But then all the women AND the men—" Clutching her chest and hitting the side of the bed, crying she screamed, "Why, why, WHY?!"

Hearing the front door open, Trish quickly dried her eyes and walked to the bathroom to fix her face. Down the hall, he walked as if he were God. Never looking at her, he opens the closet door and asks, "You made up your mind or what?"

This was the conversation she had been avoiding for a while. "Terry, why are you putting this off on me? You did this, and it's not fair!"

Coldly, he looks at her and says "Listen, I made a mistake, and now I got to fix it. You're my wife, and if you forgive me, they'll forgive me. But if you don't, they won't. You know I got some weak folk. Look, all I'm asking you to do is to help me out!"

Two things for sure were true: First, Terry was right about the people being weak because he was weak. The Bible says, "Like priest, like people." And second, Terry had made a mistake all right. He had gotten several of his people pregnant in the past, but this was the first time he couldn't hide the truth. It was no secret that Quetta, his baby's mama, was gone die. And now Mordecai was no longer just his "illegitimate child of sorts," but now he would soon be motherless. If Terry didn't do the right thing, he would lose his child and his church! You see, Terry needed Trish to go before the church and take a stand proclaiming her forgiveness of her husband and the OTHER WOMEN. He also needed Trish to ask Quetta to allow her to raise Mordecai as her own. This would be a trial for her. After all, why should she be the person going before the people when it was her husband's whorish nature that had caused all this? Nevertheless, she agreed.

Lying beside the man she thought she loved, anger began to fill her heart. The anger turned to hatred, and the hatred turned to fury. She was angry with God. She needed answers. She needed a sign from Him that what she was about to do was the best for all involved. What do you do when you desperately need an answer from God and He doesn't answer? Trish was about to find out.

The next morning she woke to find Terry was not there. She found a note he had written and left by her purse. "Gone to the church to pray."

Balling the letter up and throwing it in the trash beside the door, she thought, *That's what got me here in the first place—him and his damn praying.*

Feeling convicted, she repented and proceeded to make a pot of coffee. Looking in the refrigerator, she saw what she had seen for the past five years—no food. Maybe this will change once Quetta dies and we get the boy. You know, that's so ironic. Just a few years ago, Quetta was thinking along the same lines as well, that maybe her life would change when Trish died.

Settling on coffee and toast, she decides to call Mother Gill. Getting no answer, she starts to pray. "Father, don't leave me like this. I am growing cold, and I am starting to question even you. Help me, please, because I don't have much time left, and I don't want it to be filled with offense. Besides, Mordecai is innocent—it isn't his fault!"

Suddenly, the doorbell rings, and to her surprise, it was Mother Gill.

"Morning to you, First Lady. I came by to speak to Pastor. Is he awake yet?"

Trying to hold back her tears, Trish responds, "Yeah, but he's at the church, praying, and I don't know how long he has been there . . . or if he is still there . . . or even if he has been there at all!"

Seeing the pain in Trish's eyes, Mother asked to come in. "What's wrong child? Do you want to talk about it?"

Making a gesture for the clock, Trish responds, "No I am just pushed for time this morning."

"Okay. Well, I'll let you be for now. I'm going to run by the church and talk to Rev, if that's all right with you?"

Reaching for the couch for support during a moment of weakness, Trish responds, "Mother, that would be fine. I'll see you at Sunday school."

Mother Gill pulled up into the church lot, not surprised to find there was no one there. "Where the hell is that negro anyway? This shit has got to stop."

Terry was at Quetta's house, trying to convince her to come to church this morning and to bring Mordecai. "T, you need to get the FUCK off my porch before I call the police. What in hell are you here for anyway? We ain't seen you for the past few months, and it's been longer than that since you have sent any cheese to this address! So why don't you act like the mouse that you are and crawl the hell away?"

Seemingly sincere, Terry replies, "Boo, you've got every right to be mad at me, but I have been thinking . . . thinking about how much I love you and Mordecai. I really want you to be part of my life, and I finally found a way to make that happen."

Thinking that maybe he had changed and might be telling the truth, she slowly opened the door. "Okay, I'm listening. What, what, WHAT do you want?"

"I need you to come to the church this morning. I'm going to tell the church the truth about everything. Do you remember what I told you when I first met you?"

"Ya' damn skippy, I do!"

Attempting to appear spiritual, he takes her hand and says, "Baby, you can't be cussing like that if you're going to be the first lady and my wife."

Quetta didn't know what to think at this point. What was this fool planning? Was he just trying to get some tail, or was he being for real? Knowing him, she leans in to kiss him on the side of his neck, with her right hand on his lower stomach near his pelvic area. These were his weak spots, and if he were just on a booty call, the whore in him would quickly rise.

Knowing her as he did, he knew she would try to test him, so he took a step back and gathered himself, remembering his own philosophy: "ALL TAIL AIN'T GOOD TAIL. EVEN THOUGH YOU'RE A WHORE, KNOW WHEN TO HIT THE DOOR." Besides, he had to convince her to come to the church. "Baby, listen, I know I gave you AIDS, but Trish gave it to me."

Shouting in disbelief, Quetta said, "You're lying! I know you are! That woman loves you, man, even I know that! How is she gonna give you AIDS? Huh? The girl was a virgin when y'all got married! You're the only dick she's had, and it's your sick dick that got her sick. So don't lie!"

"Listen to me, Quetta. Do you remember when I dropped her off at chemo? You came by and saw me with Brother Price?"

Remembering the whole ordeal as if it had just happened, Quetta started to reflect on her situation and the fact that the man standing in her living room had all but ended her life. "You mean the day I came in and saw him giving you head, you sorry son of a bitch!"

"Quetta, first of all, if you had opened the bedroom door all the way, you would have seen that he was asking me to forgive 'him' for sleeping with Trish. I felt like you do right now. How could I have trusted him and he betrayed me like this? I gave him somewhere to stay, and this is how he repaid me. Baby, when you came in, I was in the process of telling him he had to get the hell out of my house, and he fell to his knees begging for forgiveness. I swear! Look, come to the church today, and I will show you that I am telling the truth. I am going to straighten out all of this. You'll see."

Terry knew he had gotten through to her. He always could tell because Quetta was a thinker, and once you broke that barrier and made her think, you had her. It didn't matter what you made her think as long as you made her think.

CHAPTER 3

Now That's the DEEEEEVIL!

Back at the church, Mother Gill, still waiting for Pastor Peters, thought it a good thing to call and encourage Quetta to come to church this morning. She couldn't quite put her hands on it, but she knew in her heart, for some reason, Quetta needed to be there. Quetta never picked up the phone. This was not the norm for her, seeing it might be her doctor with good news, saying her blood count was up. Or the adoption agency calling to say they'd found a home for Mordecai, which would have been a miracle because it's hard enough to place special needs children, let alone children with AIDS.

Quetta picked up on the second call but sounded preoccupied. "Hello, Quetta, baby. How you feeling this morning?"

Sounding aloof she responds, "Good morning, Sister Gill, how are you this morning?"

This was their signal to each other when either of them was in the midst of something and could not talk at the moment but would most definitely discuss things later. Letting Quetta know she knew who was there, Mother says, "When that bastard leaves, you need to be getting to the church! If you've got time to 'HOE,' you've got time to GO . . . And I mean to church." Before hanging up on her, Mother Gill angrily hollers through the phone, "Now kick his ass off of you, close your legs, pick your dignity off the darn floor, wash your tail, and get your filthy behind to the church!"

Feeling dirty, Quetta says to Terry, "You've got to go now. I need to be getting dressed if you want me to come to the church."

Feeling he had not lost his touch, Terry puts his clothes back on, takes a look in the mirror, and thinks to himself, *I STILL GOT IT! Everything will be back to normal in just a few hours. I can kill all these dumbass birds with one stone.*

Leaning down to kiss her on the forehead, he bids her goodbye.

"Terry, why don't you kiss me in the mouth? We both got it, and it's not like you can catch it twice, you know."

Looking back at her with contempt and disgust, trying his best to fake a smile, Terry says, "I know, sweetie, but body fluids, you know. That's why I use a rubber because I love you, and I don't want to make you sicker. I mean, you never know, huh? See you in a few."

Leaving Quetta sitting on the edge of the couch, Terry makes a quick exit to avoid further conversation. The very thing that Quetta had promised herself never to allow to happen again had occurred. Terry was a dog, and she knew it, but for some reason, she could not resist his charms. It's true what they say, when you lie down with dogs, you get up with fleas. That's what happened to her. Terry's "fleas" had infected her and Mordecai.

She could remember one day, at the age of sixteen, while sitting in service, Apostle Apax began to prophesy as the anointing fell very strong. Suddenly, Apostle points to her and says, "Daughter, stay the course, the enemy's tricky, and he's afraid of the anointing on your life."

Oddly enough, what occurred next now made so much sense to Quetta. Turning to the ministers sitting behind him in the pulpit, he beckons Terry to come and stand beside him. Turning back to her, he says, "There are demons that have been assigned to your life. So, daughter, stay in the face of God. Ask him to sharpen your discernment."

Walking over to Quetta's mother, he takes her by the hand.

"Mother Hamilton, sometimes a mother can desire the best for her children only to see the worst outcome." Squeezing her hand, he asks, "Do you understand what I'm saying to you?"

Weeping softly, with sadness in her heart, she replies, "Yes, sir."

Later that day after service, Mother Hamilton sits Quetta down to talk to her. "Quetta, I want you to promise me something. Don't make the same mistakes I did. In my youth, I forgot the Lord, but He was merciful, allowing Apostle Apax to minister healing to my broken spirit. I never imagined I would be having this conversation with you this soon. But after the confirmation from the Lord today, we need to talk. I had this same conversation with your brother just before he went to college, and it only made him hate me. So after he left, I decided to wait until you were spiritually mature enough for me to share this with you."

Quetta had only seen her mother in the light of love and respect. Was that about to change? Sitting beside her, Mother Hamilton, taking a deep breath, looking into the eyes of her only daughter, found herself faced with a difficult decision. How far could she go and how deep could she get without damaging her innocence? She knew at that moment that if she did not become transparent and remove the veil, her daughter might befall her same fate.

That's what's wrong with parents today: They are not honest with their children. There's that underlying fear that their children will hate them and/or lose their respect for them. Children need to know that mom and dad are not perfect and have made mistakes in their lifetime. Sometimes they miss the mark. If they weren't the best students, their children need to know. If drugs or alcohol played a part in the parent's life or if they got some "illegal tail" and had a child out of wedlock, they need to be honest with their children. This is what Mother Hamilton was about to do.

"Quetta, baby, when I talked to your brother, the first mistake I made was to try to justify what I did. But, baby, the truth was nobody put a gun to my head, and there's no easy way to say this. So I'm gonna just come right on out and say it. Right after I graduated from college, things were going pretty good for me. I had a degree, a place to stay, and a promising future. I got saved and became a member of Anointed Fellowship Non-Denominational Cathedral. Pastor James London was the senior pastor at that time. I was young, vulnerable, and very impressionable. Wanting to live my life in complete obedience to the Lord, I did whatever Pastor London told me to do. He could quote scripture like forty goin' north. I had never heard anyone teach the way he did. EVERYTHING he said was 'gospel' to me. Shortly after joining AFNC, Pastor London took me under his wing, and I felt so honored to have the favor of my pastor! A lot of things happened when I was at that church. Some good, some bad . . . some very, VERY BAD. It was the bad things that caused me to leave that church for good.

"Right after I left the church was when I married Thomas Hamilton. I was pregnant with you, and your brother was only two. Thomas knew that I was expecting, but he didn't care because he loved me. When we got married, people thought we rushed into it because of my condition. Thomas never once advertised the fact that the baby I was carrying wasn't his. He humbly, out of love for me, took a lot of criticism from folks, and he allowed them to defame his name. He never once shamed me, and he always treated you and your brother like his own."

Already devastated to find out that the man she had called Dad all her life was not "Dad" at all, Quetta stared at her mother in disbelief. She couldn't begin to imagine what else her mother was about to reveal. Walking over to the cedar chest, Mother Hamilton slowly removes the antique blankets and what-nots stored inside. At the bottom of the chest was a cherry wood box. Inside this Pandora's box was Quetta's identity. Smoothing her hand across the top, Mother Hamilton opens it and says, "Child, the name on this birth certificate will explain it all." Handing it to her daughter, she turned her back as tears flowed down her cheeks.

Fearing the unknown, breathing very rapidly, hands shaking, Quetta looked down at the paper. The look on Quetta's face was one of hurt, disappointment, and disbelief all wrapped up in one. How could her mother have kept this truth from her all these years? She begins to question her mother. "Mama, are you telling me that Pastor London, 'your' pastor, was my real father?! I thought he was married? And how could you keep this from me for so long? Now the man's dead! I'll never have the chance to know him.

Starting to cry, Quetta says, "I'll never be able to . . ."

Quetta slumps to her knees on the cold hardwood floor and sobs uncontrollably. She wanted to be angry. She wanted to rake her mother over the coals of shame with words of disgust and disappointment. She wanted to do and say so many things. At that very moment, Apostle Apax's voice spoke clearly in her mind, "Daughter, stay the course . . . Ask God to sharpen your discernment."

She begins to realize how much courage it took for her mother to give up this simple piece of paper. Suddenly, Quetta gathers her emotions, turns to her mother, and states, "Well, Mama, this is not so bad. Pastor London was a very nice man. I guess we all make mistakes, huh?"

Turning to face her daughter with a look of relief in her eyes, Mother Hamilton reaches for her baby girl. She looks into her eyes and then clutches her ever so closely.

Those were precious moments for Quetta and Mother Hamilton. Quetta was really hurt when her mother passed a few short years later. Looking back on that season in her life, it had become a bittersweet memory in her mind. She was grateful her mother didn't live to see the horrible mess she had made of her own life. Before her mother passed, Quetta was so full of life and had great expectations for her future. She had planned to get her degree and open her own business.

She also knew God had called her into ministry. Her mother would have been so proud.

Quetta understood now, more than ever, what Apostle Apax meant by those prophetic words spoken so long ago. She wished she could tell him how right he was, but you see, Apax just disappeared one day. No one knows what happened to him. Some thought he might have been abducted. Some thought, because of his age (he was ninety-two at the time), that he might have suddenly developed Alzheimer's and simply walked away, never to be found. That story didn't go over well because everyone knew Apax was healthy as a horse. No one knows for sure. Police never found a clue. The whole ordeal left the church wondering if Apax's wife had gone crazy. All she ever said was, "Oh, he's okay. He told me he was going on before me to make sure everything was ready before I get there."

Everyone loved her so much they just indulged her fantasies.

Afterward, Terry was appointed pastor. But, no one knew just how deeply wounded Terry was about Apax's disappearance because he never once shed a tear—not when he helped with the closed-casket funeral arrangements, not when he preached the eulogy, not even at the grave site. Some thought he was in denial. He and Apax were close, VERY close, so close that Terry's reaction had a lot of folk worried. Others thought that maybe, just maybe, he had "matured enough spiritually," that he wasn't moved by the circumstance. Maybe he was just trying to be strong for everyone else. I guess that goes to show you that you should never mistake a person's silence for strength. Apostle lived a sincere life for the Lord, and there was no need for mourning as people who have no hope after death—if you live right, you'll see Apax again.

It was after Apostle Apax's disappearance that things really began to change. Quetta got caught up with Terry and ended up having Mordecai. Having him out of wedlock left her feeling used and angry, almost to the point of no return. She had a hard time imagining that God could ever forgive her, much less use her in ministry. And now she found herself struggling from day to day, her future had gone down the drain. *Well, no use crying over spilled milk*, she thought. *Better get ready for church. Maybe Terry will do the right thing today. Just maybe, today would be the day that would change everything.*

Sitting in front of the church, Mother Gill dozed off and fell into a deep sleep. Mumbling, she started to talk in her sleep as if she was having a conversation with Apax himself and as if he was sitting right there in the car with her. "You know, Apostle, your church is going to hell in a handbasket, and it's all because of that boy of yours. Why'd you give him the church anyhow? You know he ain't no good!"

"Daughter, it never was my church. It has always been the Lord's church. No matter how bad it gets, you've got to help them because if you don't, then who will?" Right about then, the apostle turned into a chipmunk and danced off in his tutu.

Suddenly, Mother wakes up and realizes she's been dreaming. "That's the last time I eat chops from that damn store."

Tapping on the window of her car, Deamon Price informs Mother Gill that she can come into the church. Turns out, he has been in there the whole time. "How in the hell'd you get in the church, boy?"

Tossing his hand with a twitch and a twirl, "I got a key. Pastor gave it to me. I used to come by, park on the lot, and pray sometimes when I first got out of jail and the pastor noticed me sitting in my car. I told him I come every day so he gave me a key and said I could come in whenever I wanted to. Anyways, come on in."

Umph . . . grabbing her purse and Bible, Mother locks her car and walks into the church. Entering the sanctuary, she finds it necessary to answer nature's call. Deamon just sat on the front pew, where the first lady would normally sit, and smiled as if he had something to hide. From the back of the church, a voice said soft and simply, "Hey, boo." It was Terry.

Forgetting they were not alone, Deamon jumps up and rushes to the arms of his lover of the past five years. "What took you so long? I thought you had forgotten about me!"

"Naw, I had some shit to handle, but it's cool, or at least it will be. What time is it?"

Looking at his watch Deamon assures Terry there is enough time for a quickie. "It's not even 7:00 a.m. What do you have in mind, playa?"

Smiling, Terry responds, "Ohhh, I love it when you talk masculine."

Kissing each other as if man and wife, they embrace each other in the sanctuary, holding and fondling each other like schoolchildren behind the bleachers. Slowly, they began to remove each other's clothing. In the heat of passion, Terry pushes Deamon down to his knees as Mother Gill enters the sanctuary.

"Well, damn, if I had known that we had changed religion, I would have been down on my knees with my mouth open too. What in the hell is wrong with y'all? In the sanctuary! Now that's the deeeeeeeeevil!"

Pushing Deamon away, Terry explains, "It's not what you think. I was just, I mean, he was just . . . The devil made me do it."

With a twinkle in his eye, Deamon responds, "Naw, boo, DEAMON made you do it."

CHAPTER 4

Call the Po Po!

Back at the house, it took every bit of strength Trish had just to get dressed. What was wrong? Why was she so weak? And the pain was almost too much to bear. Where was Terry? Why was he so cold? She had to sit down just for a little while. Making it to the bathroom, she sat on the toilet, crying.

Looking down at her hands, she somehow found the strength to smile. For just a moment, she remembered how happy she used to be and how happy Terry had made her in times past. It seemed like just yesterday.

***

"Let me get that for you, Sister Hamilton."

Trish, desperately trying not to drop the large box of groceries, looks up to see who the "knight in shining armor" was who had come to her rescue—it was Terry Peters.

"Thanks, Minister Peters. I thought I could make it to the fellowship hall, but the closer I got to the door, the further away it looked!"

Terry grabs the box from Trish's hands. "A delicately beautiful woman like you shouldn't be carrying anything heavier than your Bible anyway." He smiles as Trish blushes and relinquishes possession of the oversized box.

She didn't think Terry even knew her name and was dumbfounded that he would say that she was beautiful.

She knew she paled next to most of the women in the church. She was somewhat introverted and really didn't have the "pizzazz" that men like Terry are accustomed to, or so she thought. Every single woman in the church was drooling over him. He was a prime "catch." He was one of the prominent ministers in the church. As a matter of fact, everyone in the church expected him to be appointed assistant pastor real soon.

He was also the most handsome man in the church: tall, smooth caramel-colored-skinned, dark wavy hair, thick brows and mustache, and a smile out of this world. He worked out regularly, so he was in tip-top shape, and his posture was perfect. In short, BROTHER WAS FINE! He dressed in designer suits and was always suited and booted. He had a real JE NE SAIS QUOIS kind of air about him that came naturally. Needless to say, to marry Minister Terry Peters would be a dream come true for any woman fortunate enough to snare him.

"Are you ready for the annual church banquet Saturday evening?" Terry asks.

"I've got a lot of responsibilities to attend to before Saturday, but I think I'll make it."

"Who are you going with?"

Blushing for the second time in just a few minutes, Trish replies, "Well, I hadn't planned on going with anyone. I was just going to support the fundraising efforts and enjoy everyone's presence."

"Would you do me the honor of allowing me to escort you to the banquet? I know it's last minute, but I didn't know until today if I would be able to get off from work to even go to the banquet. Please say yes. It would really make me happy and proud."

"I thought you and Demetta we're going together?

"Demetta and I are close, like sister and brother. But I've been praying about some things. I told the Lord I was ready to settle down. Here, lately, your face is all I see. I'd really like to get to know you better, and I think this banquet would be a great start. God has already told me that someday I would pastor my own church. I know your commitment level when it comes to ministry, and you carry yourself with great dignity. I need a woman of your caliber at my side. If you'll let me, I'd like the opportunity to win your respect and then one day maybe your love."

Overwhelmed by everything that Terry had just shared with her, Trish says, "Well, I'll have to pray about this. It's all so sudden."

Terry calmly takes Trish's hand and says, "I know what God has told me. I won't give up, Trish. You're the woman I want in my life. I'll give you a day or so to think about going to the banquet with me." Terry lowers his head like a child and says, "I hope I wasn't too forward, but I already got your number from the church secretary. Can I call you to talk later this evening?"

Still in a state of shock, Trish shyly replies, "That would be fine."

As Terry leaves the fellowship hall, Trish is in a daze. She is finally snapped back into reality as the decorating team arrives to prepare the fellowship hall for the upcoming banquet.

For the next two days, Terry calls Trish, politely asking her for an answer. Finally, Friday rolls around, the day before the banquet, and she agrees to go. Well, as fate would have it, they had a great time. One year later, they were married. Trish had cold feet at the last minute but somehow got up the courage to proceed with the wedding. For about two years, things were good. She couldn't even remember what happened that could have been the catalyst for all the changes in Terry's attitude. But then again, it all seemed to be centered on Apostle Apax's disappearance. Whatever triggered the change in Terry had caused him to be uncaring and heartless. The old Terry was almost nowhere to be found. Their marriage was a nightmare, and it didn't seem to bother Terry at all. It was as if he was completely oblivious to what was going on.

Trish shakes her head and begins to prepare for church. Standing to wash her hands, she notices a blemish on her jaw and tries to remember if she had fallen.

Don't be ridiculous, she thought.

Who in the world could fall and not remember it? Had she bumped herself in the night? But wouldn't she remember? The blemish was painful too! Maybe it's just a cancer spot. Putting it to the back of her mind, she proceeded to fix her face and do her makeup. It had to be perfect. Terry had given her instructions to put on extra mascara to give the "Tammy Faye" effect, so she loaded it on.

Getting into her car, she realized that she had left her Bible. "The way I feel, I'll just share with someone else!"

Driving down the expressway, she turns on the radio to listen to some jazz just to calm her nerves. Her cell phone rings, and it's Mother Gill. "Baby, where are you? You need to be getting down to the church as soon as possible."

In the background, Trish could hear Terry and Deamon yelling for her to hang up the phone and not to come.

"What's wrong? Is everything okay? Has something happened? Has Terry been hurt?"

"Not yet, but if you don't get down here, I'm gone catch a charge!"

Hanging up the cell phone, Mother Gill stands there looking at the two of them covered in shame. Too upset to say a word, she simply walks up to the pulpit and sits in Apax's chair. Taking a deep breath, she starts to hum a song. In fact, it was Apostle Apex's favorite song. "Come on out that corner, why you trying to hide?"

"Father, what has happened to your children? Don't they fear you no more? They've gotten up and started acting like the children of Israel in Psalms 106. They've forgotten you and gone astray. Lord, what are you going to do about all this here?"

As Mother Gill continued her conversation with God, a screeching sound was heard outside of the church and then a car door slamming. Terry and Deamon know what that meant and who that was.

Looking at each other, both were wondering who would be the one to break the news to Trish. They kind of giggled at each other as if to say, "Well, it's over now!" as one song writer put it. Running inside the church, barely catching her breath, Trish slams into the sanctuary to find her husband half-dressed, standing next to the church "homo," and Mother sitting in Apax's chair fast asleep.

"Terry, what's going on, and why in the hell do I have the feeling I am not going to like what I hear? Uh, not again. It was hard to accept the other women and act stupid, but all these men . . . I can't do this no more."

Feeling used, Deamon looks at Terry with tears in his eyes, having believed his lie for the past five years. Terry insisted that Deamon had been his first and ONLY experience with a man. Deamon shouts "I hate you boy...I REALLY HATE YOU THIS TIME!"

"Look, it's almost time for Sunday school, and the saints will be here soon. Why don't we talk about all this after service?" says Terry, trying to salvage what was left of the situation.

"Do you think I am actually going to stay in this place knowing what went on this morning and why Mother was about to be carted off to jail? Terry, I told you if this happened again, I was through!"

With his hands on his hips Deamon says, "And I know you don't think I'm gonna sing for your dumbass either. I can't believe you, boy! How you gonna do your boo like this?"

Without thinking, Trish lunges for Deamon, holding to his throat for dear life. It was as if she wanted to make him pay for every evil thing that Terry had done to her.

By this time, Mother Gill awoke and shouted, "He ain't worth it! The boy ain't worth it, girl! Let that 'em go! Now get to the bathroom, fix your darn face, straighten out your clothes, and leave these demons to me." Reaching for her purse, she says, "I GOT THIS!"

Remembering a scene from a local play, both men feared for their lives thinking, *Mother has a gun in her purse.*

"First of all, I don't have time to fix all this. In fact, I don't have to . . . When God gets through with both of you, you're gonna wish somebody had shot your asses! Terry, get to your office and do what you do best—pretend to be HOLY. Hell, you do that every Sunday. And as for you, boy, get on your knees at this alta right now and start calling on the Lord before you have to start calling for the PoPo!"

Then mother pulled her weapon out of her purse: HER BIBLE.

CHAPTER 5

Who's That Calling Me?

Trish had taken all that she could take and was at the point of giving up.

She understood what her pastor had taught her when she was a young girl being forced by her mother every Sunday to get her hind tail up and ready for church. The curse does not come without a cause. But what had she done to cause this curse to come upon her? What?

Sitting there, all she could think about was the look on Terry's face that pierced her heart like a knife, as well as the look on that punk's face. "How dare he do this after I took him into my home and gave him a place to stay? I must be out of my damn mind. Momma told me not to trust anyone whose perfume is sweeter and whose switch is faster than mine."

Right about then, the painful reality of what had just taken place began to manifest its dirty little head in the form of extreme weakness in her body. Fighting the urge to bust through the door with her gun in her hand and blow the hell out of them, she began to weep.

She heard a soft voice calling to her. "Daughter . . . Daughter . . ."

Thinking it was Mother Gill, wiping her tears, she prepared to face the only person who had understood her pain for the past few years. Not really realizing that Mother Gill was still in the sanctuary, she was about to receive the answer she had long awaited for.

"Daughter . . . dry your tears, I have not forgotten about you. Though it seems you are alone, I am with you."

Standing there, the reality sunk in that it was NOT Mother Gill beaconing her. It was Father God coming to see about her. "Master, if You don't help me, I won't be able to do this. I have a gun in my purse right now and no reason to live. Besides, who would miss me anyway? The man You gave me has given himself to so many others, and now I'm dying on the inside." Beating her chest, she falls to her knees and reaches inside of her purse for her gun. Putting the gun to her temple, she reminds God, "You swore You'd never leave me, so why in hell haven't You been there? WHY? WHY?!"

Remembering the words her mother spoke to her when she had been diagnosed with cancer, sitting on the side of the bed, holding her mother's hand, looking down at a face that refused to give up even to the end, it was almost as if she were reliving her mother's final moments. "Baby, don't ever charge God foolishly. The fault is never in Him. We've got to understand that all things work together for the good of them that love Him. And I know you love Him . . . don't you?"

Fighting the answer that was apparent in her spirit, Trish sighs and surrenders, knowing that her mother was correct. And as quickly as the moment came, it passed.

Meanwhile, back in the sanctuary, Mother Gill tries to reason with Deamon. "Boy, what in the hell's wrong with you?! Don't you know anything? Didn't you learn anything in jail?" Taking a breath, Mother Gill kneels beside Deamon. "Well, don't you have anything to say for yourself? I see the tears, so I know you're listening. That's the problem with young folk today. You've been bamboozled, hoodwinked, twisted all up in the mind. Don't you know sin will take you further than you want to go and keep you longer than you want to stay?"

Looking up at Mother Gill, Deamon says to her, "I ain't never asked nobody to forgive me. I ain't asked nobody to feel sorry for me, and I sure don't need your pity. All you so-called church folks, supposed to be so holy, and all y'all doing more shit than the folks in the jail." Biting her tongue, Mother Gill decided to let him talk because she understood if you let a fool talk long enough, he'd hear just how foolish he sounds. Standing up, with his hands on his hips, Deamon decides to be real with this old lady. "You know, when I first got out, I swore I was gonna try to do right. But every time I turned around, if they weren't calling me a faggot, they was calling me a sissy. And the ones that weren't talking were trying to get up on this. And I ain't talking about the women either. Not one time did any one of you ask me if I needed prayer. But I'm straight though."

Feeling that this was the perfect time to pray with him, Mother Gill stands and places her hand on his shoulder. With a loud yell, as if someone had dumped acid on his shoulders, Deamon yanks himself away from her and screams, "NO!" What had actually happened was that the anointing flowing from Mother Gill's touch was so powerful that the demon in Deamon knew that he had to get away. "I don't need you. I don't want you." And in a high-pitched voice, he steps toward her and screams, "I HATE YOU!"

As Mother Gill realizes that she doesn't have any bullets in her gun, she slowly backs away and says, "All right then, son. I'll leave you to yourself and God." Walking to the choir room, she again starts to hum Apostle Apax's favorite song, "O' Sinner, Why You Tryin' to Hide."

"Delroy . . . Delroy."

Not realizing he was speaking out loud, in fear, Deamon swings around and screams, "What the hell?"

You see, Delroy was Deamon's real name. And the only person who knew his real name was his grandmother who had been dead for the past twelve years. His grandmother raised him until the age of ten after his mother left him with her one night and never returned. For his tenth birthday, his father Derrick showed up on Meema's porch, shouting, "I want my son. You can't keep him from me, old bitch! His mama's dead, or she might as well be. And I'm the only family he's got."

Long story short, the courts forced Meema to hand him over. For Delroy, things only got worse. As soon as he had his son in his clutches, he began to molest him, teaching him things no father should ever teach his son. Slowly but surely, everything that Meema instilled in his sweet little innocent spirit about the love of God was replaced with hatred. He tried praying, on his knees like she taught him, only to be mocked by his father. "Well, as long as you're down there, you might as well make me happy."

You see, Delroy had not only been born into a perverted bloodline, but he was also being formed into a life that would drive him further away from God. Thinking things could not get worse, one Saturday night, in a drunken stupor, his father entered his bedroom with a friend and said, "Delina, this is David. David, this is Delina. Now I want you to make him happy too."

With tears in his eyes, he begged his father, "Please, Daddy, no... NO PLEASE".

Turning as if he heard nothing, he leaves the room and locks the door. All that could be heard was a little boy losing what was left of his innocence as he prayed aloud, "Jesus, make it stop. Jesus, make it stop."

Over and over, he was raped by this man called David. And still, things got worse. The following Sunday, Delroy thought if he could get to church, he could see his Meema and tell her the terrible things that had been happening to him. Instead, his father dressed him in a black skirt and black blouse and made up his face with makeup. He couldn't walk in heels so his father gave him a pair of black penny loafers. Smoothing back his dark and waving hair, he told Delroy, "All you've got to say is 'I've got a surprise for you.'"

He took him to the corner of Kimbrum and Follister and sold him over and over at a price. What broke his little heart was that his very first "john" was a deacon from Meema's church. Deacon Broady never recognized Delroy because of the makeup and the clothes. Mixed with white genes from his mother and black from his father, Delroy passed for the cutest little girl one would ever see.

Kneeling in the sanctuary, tears began to flood Deamon's eyes as the painful memories lingered in his mind, refusing to leave. "Jesus, make it stop. Please make it stop!" It was as if Deamon was that innocent little boy on his knees in his father's bedroom again.

"Delroy . . . Delroy, if you let me, I can heal your heart. If you trust me, I can take away the pain. It wasn't your fault."

Feeling a sense of peace, Delroy wipes the tears from his eyes and heads for the choir room to ask Mother Gill to pray for him.

CHAPTER 6

Who Would Have Thought?

Sitting in his office, with his face in his hands, Terry stops and realizes what a mess he has made. "Damn. I done fucked up now. What am I gone do? I've got to fix this."

"Terry . . . Terry."

"What do You want with me now?! I told You, I don't want You. I don't need You. I've got this! It isn't like it used to be." Hitting his desk, he grabs his Bible and shakes it in the air and shouts, "THIS DOESN'T WORK NO MORE!"

You see, Terry knew the voice of God, and he once walked very close with Him. But he forgot what Deuteronomy 8:18 said about forgetting God who gives him the power to get wealth.

"Let me tell you something. When I got this church, they didn't have but two deacons, one and a half church mothers, four choir members, and six faithful folk. I DID THIS. These folk come to see me because

I've got what they need. People don't care about God anymore. So You need to get off my back."

On the other side of the wall, Mother Gill could hear Terry ranting and raving, swearing and cursing like a sailor. She simply moved to the other side of the room because she felt like, "When God strikes that fool down, I don't want to get no smoke on my clothes."

"Terry . . . Terry."

Shouting at the top of his lungs, he yells, "Leave me alone! All those church folks did was use me. They had me cutting the grass, cleaning toilets, driving the church van, and all that crazy shit FOR FREE! Never once did those fools say thank you. Every time I turned around, the church needs this . . . the church needs that. Annual day for this . . . annual day for that. Offering for this . . . offering for that. Hell, the only person I ever saw get rich was the damn pastor. He was driving a champagne-colored Caddy, all pimped out and shit, and the heifer he was married to wasn't any better. The wench wouldn't even speak to the very folks that bought HER the damn suits she had on, with her old stinking ass. So why the hell do I need to be like one of those SNAKES? I'm just being real with mine!

"And then YOU . . . You bring me over here to 'Holy Land House of Prayer.' You give me a real man of God and then take him away. Apax was the only pastor I ever had worth the salt in his bread. He was the closest to **You** I ever got, and then You go and take him away from me and expect me to do good? Why HIM?"

"TERRY . . . TERRY."

Shouting at the top of his lungs, Terry responds, "NO, GOD! I'm through. I'm through listening. I'm doing this my way. You hear me? MY WAY!"

In the choir room, curiosity overwhelms Mother Gill, and she presses her ear to the wall and continues to listen to Terry's foolishness. Shaking her head, she begins rocking back and forth as she talks to God.

"Lord, I never thought I'd see the day when I was the holiest thing in the church house." Ha, ha! Mother Gill laughs remembering her days of short skirts, fast cars, hot men, and all night juke joints. "What would Mama think of me now? Who would have thought the bastard child would turn out to be a blessing? Um, um, um, well, what am I gone do now, Father? This one is too big for me." Memories of what happened to her husband over fifty years ago brought tears to her eyes.

Standing over the body of the man her husband Charlie had killed during a fight over **his** wife, she could still smell the smoke from the gun and see the rage in her husband's eyes as he took the life of this innocent man. That day, she saw something in the eyes of her husband that she had never seen before—passion. But not for her. It was for Liyla, who was wrapped in a sheet in the corner, eyes big as silver dollars, shocked as hell, babbling to herself. Standing there, Mother Gill, who was just Mattie then, had a choice to make: lie for her no-good husband or tell the truth on her no-good husband. Either way, she had lost HER NO-GOOD HUSBAND.

You see, back then, it was common practice to stay with a man, even though you knew he wasn't the most faithful person in the world.

"You never air your dirty laundry in the streets." Mattie could still hear her mother preaching, "What happen in this house stay in this house!"

What in the world was she gone do now? With all the commotion going on, she knew it wouldn't be long before the paddy wagon came.

"Mattie, Mattie," Charlie called.

But she couldn't hear. Standing there frozen, it was a wonder that the tears didn't freeze to her face. Being filled with hate and sorrow, Mattie began to pray, "Father, I don't know why this is happening, and I really don't have time for You to explain. You need to come on now. Get me out of this mess, and You won't have to get me out of this mess NO MORE!"

Right about then, they all heard the sound of beating on the door. "One of you niggers open this door!"

"Mattie. Mattie! What gone say? What you gone tell 'em? Jail ain't no place for a colored man."

With contention in her heart and a look of disdain, Mattie rolled her eyes and walked to the door to let the officers in.

All that could be heard was "Nigga, don't move! Nigga, get down! Nigga, drop your gun!"

By then, Officer Widlow, who was a local Uncle Tom, had entered the house. (For those of you who don't know what that is, he was the token-colored police officer because they had to have at least one.)

"What in the hell have you spooks done now?"

All of a sudden, forgetting her pain, Mattie was filled with a new rage. *How in the hell is this sorry-ass negro gone come in this house talkin' to us like this, when he's a nigga too?* she thought.

Standing there dumbfounded, Charlie, Mattie's husband, never said a word. And Liyla was still babbling and crying in the corner.

"Officer, this is Liyla, my prayer partner from the church. We received word that her husband was whippin' up on her again. When we got here, we were sure he was about to kill her. My husband, who works for Mayor Gardner, had his gun on him and told him to get off of her. The next thing I knew, he was charging like a mad man after my husband. So he pulled out his gun and shot him. That's when you got here."

Knowing Mattie from local church services, Officer Widlow was sure she was telling the truth. "You all say the same thang?"

Never saying a word, they nodded and agreed.

Officer Widlow shouted at them, as if speaking to children, "Speak up, boy!"

"Yes, sir . . . that's what happened."

"All right then. If one of you niggers can write, you gonna have to write it down on this here paper so we can get outta here."

Mattie didn't know what bothered her more: the sickening truth of her lies or the fact that the life of an innocent colored man was worth so little. Standing there, she watched as they wrapped his body up in a sheet with little respect, carried him out, and was in and out in less than an hour, never asking another question. It was then that Mattie realized that a religious look can get you out of a multitude of troubles. As long as you look the part, the **world** will pardon your sins.

To add insult to injury, forty-five years later, Mattie is forced to bury a man she never got to enjoy. You see, a week after the murder, Charlie packed his stuff and left with Liyla. Only thing was he never gave Mattie her divorce, and so she never remarried. When Mattie got the call that Charlie had died in his sleep somewhere in Chicago, she was told she had to bury him because she was still legally Mrs. Charlie Gill.

CHAPTER 7

And You Thought You Knew!

"Hey, Mattie! Sing us a song, girl!"

Leaning on the bar, drunk as a skunk and full of despair, she stumbles to the center of the juke joint where there was a mic sitting on a wooden chair. Though only a few minutes had passed, to Mattie, it seemed like a lifetime. With thoughts of Charlie, Liyla, and a life gone sour, she picks up the mic and takes a seat. Silence filled the room because when Mattie sang, she sang.

There was Mattie, sitting in the middle of a room full of people, long milky legs, crossed ever so gently, mic in one hand, cigarette in the other. Taking a puff, she begins to hum. Searching for a familiar face in the crowd, she realizes she doesn't know a soul. Stopping midriff, tears begin to flow from her eyes. Trying her best to see clearly through the tears, she spots a high yellow sugar daddy. She always was a fool for a pretty fella. Wiping her tears, smudging her mascara, she looks at him and says in a deep sultry voice, "You want to hear Mattie sing?"

When he realizes that Mattie's talking to him, he puts down his drink but doesn't say a word. Uncrossing her long legs, she stands and walks toward him. Approaching his table, she stops and squats, legs spread wide open, revealing just enough too.

"Did you hear that? A heart just skipped a beat. I said, do you want to hear me sing?"

Leaning forward, looking deep into her eyes, he says, "Sing, mama, sing."

Standing up, she softly brushes his cheek and says, "That's cool, papa," and starts to sing "Good Morning, Heart Ache."

Finishing her song, she sashays to the table in her silky satin dress; blue was always her color. Leaning over, showing every bit of her God-given cleavage, she whispers, "You got a name?"

Leaning in close enough to feel her every breath, he replies, "Perry. Perry Love."

"Um. Pretty Perry. You got a woman?"

Never skipping a beat, he replies, "I DO NOW."

All it took for Mattie to get her man was a song and a squat.

Before long, Mattie and Perry were an item. You wouldn't see one without the other. In fact, they kept company so much that Perry thought it best that Mattie take up residence with him.

While singing one day, Mattie fainted at the juke joint. Rushing to her aid, heart racing with fear, Perry carries her to a chair. Boy, you should have seen the expression on onlookers faces. Everybody was sure of what was going on. Mattie was in the "family way." Before you knew it, she had to fold her pretty blue satin dress up and put it away in her top drawer. It would be nine months before she could wear it again. Seven months later, to be exact, Zachary was born.

Cutting to the chase, there was a knock at the door. "Miss Mattie! Miss Mattie! Come quick now!"

Mattie, unsure of what was happening, grabbed her over coat and rushed out the door with Toby. It was as if life was playing a cruel joke on her. Perry and Zach, on their way home from the market, had run off the road over into the creek and drowned. Now Mattie was SURE to have a breakdown. Never having the opportunity to enjoy Charlie, now she was without Perry as well. And mercy, Jesus, Zachary was only two years old. Looking up to the sky, ferociously shaking clenched fists at God, she screamed at the top of her lungs, "I hate You! I HATE You! I HATE YOU!"

It was then that Mattie promised herself never to love again. Everything she ever loved left her.

Sitting in the choir room, all these memories flooded Mother Gill's heart. Somehow, deep within, she understood. Oddly enough, she had been in Trish, Terry, and Deamon's position before. You would really be surprised to know who has been molested in this world.

Back in his office, mumbling, Terry visualized himself standing in Pastor Buck's office, crying like a girl. *How could this man be accusing me of sleeping with his wife? Damn! I didn't even piss unless he told me to,* Terry thought. *And he gone come at me like this?! All those fuckin' years of cleaning toilets, washing cars, paying other folks bills with MY rent money, just because Buck said so. I must have been out of my GOD DAMMED mind!* **So-called church folk.** *That bastard wasn't saved. He was nothing but a religious pimp prostituting my anointing, abusing my loyalty, despising my youth. The low-down dirty nigkka!*

Terry's foolishness left his heart as he verbally rebukes God. "Buck was jealous of me. I know he was. And You knew it, and You didn't do a damn thing about it.

"Well, God . . . you ain't saying nothing! Talk to me. Say something! TALK TO ME, DAMN IT!" Terry, filled with rage, demanded that God speak. "You talk to that old woman Gill. You talked to Apax! Hell, You even talk to Trish with her old ignorant ass. I knew You weren't for real because if You were, this wouldn't be happening." Screaming at the top of his lungs, fist clinched and bolled up pounding on his desk, he yells one final time, "I said talk to me!"

Suddenly, Terry hears the voice of God. "All right! You want to talk? Let's talk. But let's talk about your transgressions, your iniquities, your whorish nature, your lying, your backbiting, your thievery, your fornications, your adultery, your blasphemy, your lusting, your hypocrisy, your hatred, your jealousy, your violent nature, your abusive nature, your neglect, your sexual immorality, your emulations, your envy, your sowing seeds of discord, your lasciviousness, your gluttony, your demonic relationships, your admissions, your omissions, your faithLESSness. And if that's not enough, let's talk about your failure to feed My sheep, your failure to obey My commandments, your failure to pay your tithes, your failure to study My word, your failure to hear My voice, your failure to love your wife, your failure to love your children, your failure to honor your vows. And on top of all of this, you have the audacity to charge Me foolishly. You wanted Me to speak? SO NOW I SPEAK! But I speak in judgment."

Suddenly, Terry realizes he had crossed the line. Remembering the swift judgment that came upon Nabal in 1 Samuel 25:2–38, fear fell upon him. He could hear Apostle Apax quoting his favorite passage of scripture in Acts 17:28, "IN HIM WE LIVE, AND MOVE, AND HAVE OUR BEING!"

It was finished. Terry didn't have to worry about having a conversation with God anymore. All of a sudden, all the transgressions, iniquities, whorish nature, lying, backbiting, thievery, fornications, adultery, blasphemy, lusting, hypocrisy, hatred, jealousy, violent nature, abusive nature, neglect, sexual immorality, emulations, envy, sowing seeds of discord, lasciviousness, gluttony, demonic relationships, admissions, omissions, faithlessness, his failure to feed God's sheep, his failure to obey God's commandments, his failure to pay his tithes, his failure to study God's word, his failure to hear God's voice, his failure to love his wife, his failure to love his children, his failure to honor his vows, and the charging of God foolishly, *ALONG WITH HIS HEART*, all stopped!

All at once, every sin committed in his body flashed before his eyes. Clutching his chest, falling to the floor, Terry reaches toward the bookcase to break his fall and only touches it with his fingertips. And just like the flock he had led all these years, the bookcase crashes to the floor, scattering the books abroad. The crashing sound echoed throughout the walls as a deep, dark silence fell throughout every room of the church.

JUDGMENT HAD COME!

In one room was a soul praying to die yet deserving to live and in another room a soul deserving to die, yet feeling they had the right to live. Dropping the gun, Trish followed the sound of the crash. Snapping back into reality, Mother Gill hastens to Terry's office and Deamon stops abruptly in his tracks and heads toward the pastor's office as well. Entering the room together, the sight of Terry's body stretched out on the floor, covered in books, eyes and mouth wide open, was a sight that neither one of them would forget for the rest of their lives.

Shocking, isn't it? How one unlikely event can answer the prayers of so many . . . Surely, no one wanted Terry dead, but God's judgment is JUST! God knew that Terry's lies would destroy the lives of these precious souls. God promises to never put on us more than we can bear. Knowing they wouldn't be able to bear the burden of Terry's sinful lies, and that each of them would surely break, He allowed death to heal ALL their wounds.

Trish had received her answer for help. No longer having the pressure of dealing with a whorish, self-centered husband, just like Abigail, she was free from the pain of all her husband's sins.

And Deamon, having prayed for Jesus to make it stop, had received his request as well. With Terry's death came the beginning of his healing process.

And then there was Mother Gill's prayer for God to put a stop to all this madness.

Adultery, homosexuality, suicidal thoughts, and immorality are the visual prisons that we see in each individual here, yet we passed judgment before we knew their painful history.

QUICK QUESTION:

Why is it that MAN has to know YOUR painful past for him to validate YOUR actions?

Finishing their pork chops, greens, mashed potatoes, gravy, and a big jar of Kool-Aid, Mother Gills looks across the table at Pearleene's shocked, wild-eyed, and bewildered face. Placing a big plate of peach cobbler and homemade ice cream in front of her from Sunday, she says, "Baby, close your mouth . . ."

HUMPH . . . AND YOU THOUGHT YOU KNEW CHURCH FOLKS? CHILD, I'M JUST GETTING STARTED!

ENDORSEMENTS

When I started reading this book, I couldn't put it down until I finished it. *So You Think You Know Church Folk?* is an eye-opener and a sad reflection to a large percentage of black churches. Be prepared to think because this book is going to take you there.

Elder W. Scott
New Growth in Christ, Memphis, Tennessee

Now that'll preach!!!
- **Apostle Michelle H. Ucheoma approves this message.**

WHY THIS BOOK
WAS WRITTEN

Shalom, beloved!

I wanted to again take this time to thank every one of you for your support. When I endeavored to write this book, there were mixed emotions and comments. Those who ACTUALLY READ the book gave wonderful reviews, but those who HAD NOT read the book and heard only the topic kicked against such a book even being published. On one hand, some said, "You are going to make the black churches look bad!" And on the other, some said, "I could care less about what happens in the BLACK CHURCHES!" Let me be the first to say that this book is not purely based on any one particular race, creed, religion, or denomination. Regardless of what denomination you are affiliated with, there are those who abuse their passions. This book was not to defame the church in any way. It is only to shed light on what is prevalent in the body of Christ that NO ONE IS WILLING TO ADDRESS OPENLY!

While speaking to one of the naysayers, his response was very clear: "As long as it is not happening in OUR CHURCHES, let them kill each other for all we care. If they are not smart enough to vote that damn pastor out, then that's on them."

Sitting there, the realization came that it was even more important for me to push through the adversities as I fought for my vision because not only did we have those inside our assemblies fighting against each other and seeking our own demise but we had those on the outside of our assemblies as well who were sitting on the sidelines waiting for us to destroy ourselves. This naysayer's response was as such: "Less work for us."

To that individual, I must say, "What Satan meant for our bad, FATHER GOD meant for our good."

God simply used you to confirm my mission. So thank you soooooooooooooo much for all your negative words.

Now to those that abide on the inside of our assemblies, who have a problem with this series of books (Oh yes, there is much more to come!) and you find yourself offended, let me help you! The word of God says in 1 Timothy 5:22b, "***Neither be not partaker of other men's sins: keep thyself pure.***"

If you are aware of things such as these going on in your assembly, and you say nothing, you are also guilty of the same offenses. You might disagree, but you can't argue with the word.

Revelations 18:4–9

"And I heard another voice from heaven, saying, Come out of her, my people, that ye be not partakers of her sins, and that ye receive not of her plagues. For her sins have reached unto heaven, and God hath remembered her iniquities. Reward her even as she rewarded you, and double unto her double according to her works: in the cup which she hath filled fill to her double. How much she hath glorified herself, and

lived deliciously, so much torment and sorrow give her: for she saith in her heart, I sit as queen, and am no widow, and shall see no sorrow. Therefore shall her plagues come in one day, death, and mourning, and famine; and she shall be utterly burned with fire: for strong [is] the Lord God who judgeth her. And the kings of the earth, who have committed fornication and lived deliciously with her, shall bewail her, and lament for her, when they shall see the smoke of her burning."

If you allow this to happen without shouting, **"The emperor has no clothes!"** you will one day find yourself standing before Father NAKED!

To the emperors guilty of these atrocities, <u>SIMPLY STOP!</u>

Use the "My Experiences" pages to write down the various things you have gone through. Use the "My `Victories" pages to write down how you overcame the various experiences you have had.

MY CHURCH HURT EXPERIENCES

If you have more to write, get as much paper as you need. It's important to write it <u>ALL</u> down. Send us the **"My Experiences & My Victories"** pages as a spiritual signal to God that you are "casting your cares upon him."

MY CHURCH HURT VICTORIES AND RECOVERIES

Write testimonies of how you overcame
the experiences you have had.
Give God thanks for every victory! <u>You made it!</u>

I "cast" each experience, every care, upon You, Lord, and decree that I am no longer bound or controlled by them. I am free from the consequences and the effects of my past. I have the victory, and I am healed! Amen!

Signature

Date

Forward to:
Paula Ferguson Ministries
PFERGUSONMINISTRIES@OUTLOOK.COM or
PFERGMIN@OUTLOOK.COM

MY MAP TO VICTORY

Whenever you use a recipe, there are specific measurements, ingredients, and directions that must be followed to obtain the same positive result every time. It's only when you deviate from the recipe that results change. I am providing this section for you, as God delivers you out of future happenstances, to create your own recipe for deliverance. Make note of every divine revelation, every instruction given, every lesson learned, and every movement made that led to the manifestation of your deliverance. Keep this section in a safe place to reflect back on using it as a **Map to Victory.**

PRAYER OF THE ABUSED

Father God, I know that in this life many things can happen to me. I know that at times I may feel that I have received an unfair amount of persecution, hurt, and pain. But, Father, I acknowledge today that all these things have worked and continue to work for my good because I love You, and I am called according to YOUR purpose. I forgive every person who was an instrument of hurt, persecution, or pain in my life. I understand that by predestination, every person was in my life to help me to grow spiritually. I understand that to evolve spiritually, there must be positive and negative experiences. The greater the experience, the greater the evolution. I thank You, Father, that You counted me worthy of each and every trial, tribulation, and temptation. I thank You even more that by Your love, wisdom, grace and strength, I have come **through** them. I am not a victim but a victor. I am victorious in every situation, and I bring You glory because my life is a living testimony of Your power to deliver and Your wisdom to know just how much I can endure. I thank You for the understanding that before the foundation of the world, I was predestined to come through every test victorious. By Your grace, I overcame by the blood of the Lamb of God, Jesus Christ, and by the words of my testimony. I know that there is no **test**imony without a **test**. I thank You that my victories continuously strengthen me and increase my faith. I am being transformed into the image of Christ. I am the manifested son of the living God! Thank You, Lord! In Jesus's name. Amen.

A PRAYER OF THE ABUSER

If you see yourself in the confines of the pages of this book and realize that in times past, you yourself have been the abuser, pray this prayer of repentance, knowing that God is able and willing to forgive.

Father God, in the name of Jesus, You said in 1 John 1:9, that if I confess my sins, You are faithful and just to forgive me and to continuously cleanse me of my sins. I confess that I have acted in a way that has caused hurt and pain in others' lives. I have abused my gifts and prostituted them for my own causes. I have neglected to seek Your face to ensure my actions would not drastically alter another person's life in a devastating way. I desire to change. I thank You for forgiveness of sins—past, present, and future. I thank You for loving me in spite of my shortcomings. I thank You for opening my eyes to see just how I have been an instrument of hurt to the people You have entrusted to my care. I thank You for the word of God that enables me to experience a change in my life. **I decree that today I begin a new life**. I WILL allow You to begin to change my character, my thinking, and my attitude so that I will no longer be an instrument in satan's hands. I give You permission to work in me to have the will and to do the things that please You and that will help me fulfill my divine mission in the earth. You sent me here for a purpose. You gave me gifts to fulfill that purpose, and I have abused them. I pray for each person who was negatively influenced or hurt by my actions. Deliver them, strengthen them, and heal them. I thank You, Lord, for another chance to live a life pleasing to You. In Jesus's name. Amen.

MY CHURCH STORIES

Please take some time and share with us some of your "church stories"— things that you have seen that should not have happened in your religious assembly. By sharing these observations, others will know that they are not the only ones seeing and hearing the atrocities that are infecting and, thus, destroying the lives of so many men, women, and children. Forward these stories with your "My Experiences" and" My Victories" pages. Thank you!

SPECIAL THANKS

Our deepest gratitude to the following individuals and organizations who helped make this vision possible. Without their input, prayers, love, and inspiration, we would not have been able to press toward the mark of completing this first book. Thanks so very much, and God bless!

Foreword by:
Apostle Craig Ferguson, Texas
Elder Will Scott, Tennessee
Apostle Michelle Ucheoma, Wisconsin

Special thanks to our publisher:
The entire Xlibris staff for your professionalism
and for making the publishing process easy

All those who provided endorsements
Thanks for your honest reviews of this book

<u>Family and friends</u>
Who witnessed and waited patiently with me through every
heartfelt contraction as we labored to give birth to this book.

<u>Much gratitude for the prayers of the saints</u>
Who understood the need for this book to
bring healing to the Body of Christ.

SO YOU THINK ...
YOU'VE BEEN HURT?

CPSIA information can be obtained
at www.ICGtesting.com
Printed in the USA
LVHW111326190522
718764LV00015B/10

9 781669 823186